If you had to choose, would you rather be a black bear or a black mamba?

A black bear
is a mammal.

mammal

From the Author of Who Would Win?

JERRY PALLOTTA

WHAT WOULD YOU RATHER BE?

A BLACK BEAR OR A BLACK MAMBA?

SCHOLASTIC

Which sister would you rather be?
Iolanda or Silvana?

Library of Congress Cataloging-in-Publication Data available
ISBN 978-1-339-03558-1
10 9 8 7 6 5 4 3 2 1 26 27 28 29 30
Printed in the U.S.A. 40
First edition, February 2026
Book design by Jaime Lucero

A black mamba is a reptile.

A black bear
is a bear.

A black mamba
is a snake.

This black bear has black fur.

A black mamba is usually silver or gray.

It is easy to see how the black bear got its name.

The black mamba is named for its black mouth.

A black bear has two front legs and two back legs.

4 3 2 1

A black mamba does not have any arms or legs.

A black bear walks
and runs.

A black mamba slithers.

A black bear can climb trees.

A black mamba can also climb trees.

These are
black bear footprints.

These are black mamba tracks.

This is a
black bear face.

This is a black mamba face.

A black bear smells with its nose.
nose

A black mamba smells with its forked tongue.

A black bear has big, sharp teeth.

A black mamba has long, skinny fangs.

A black bear eats berries, fish, grasses, and insects.

A black mamba eats small animals.

A black bear chews its food.

A black mamba swallows its food whole.

A black bear has a short, stubby tail.

A black mamba is shaped like a long tail.

So which would you rather be? A black bear? Or a black mamba?